Easy Tuna Cookbook

50 Delicious Tuna Recipes

By
BookSumo Press

Published by
http://www.booksumo.com

Table of Contents

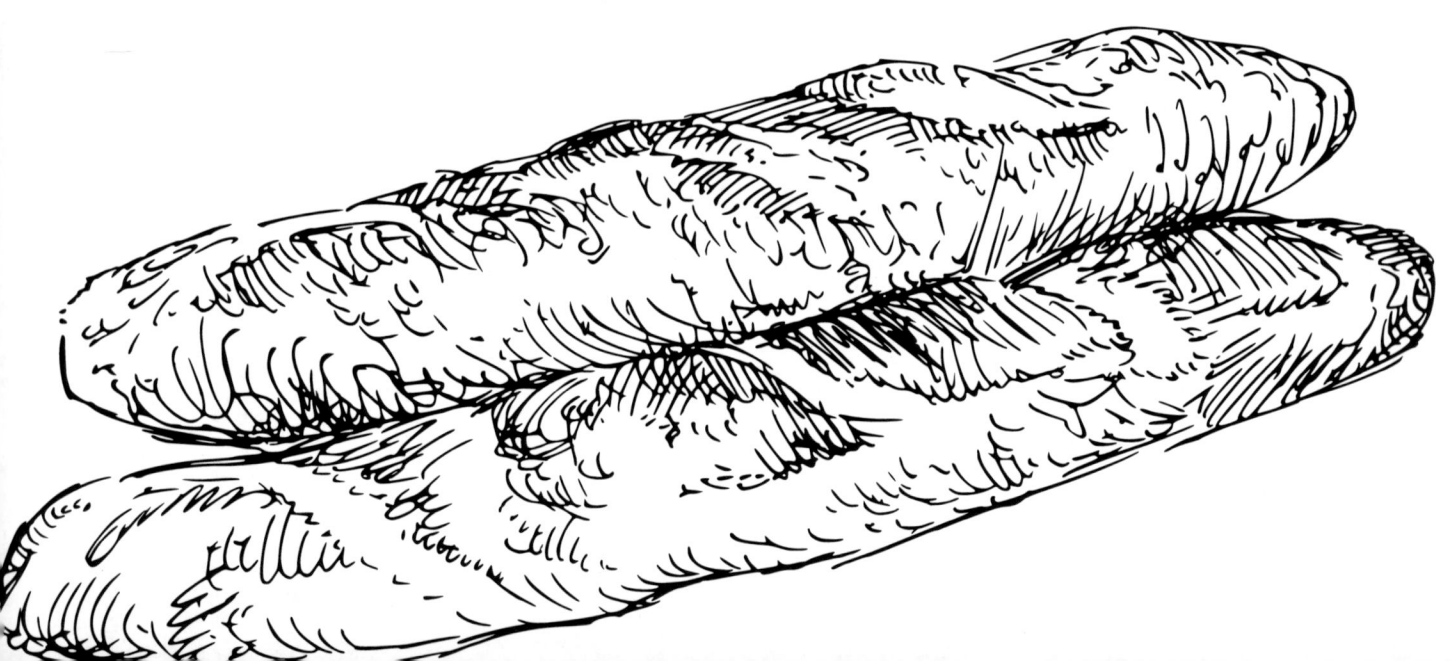

Homemade
Japanese Tuna Roll Sushi

Prep Time: 40 mins

Total Time: 1 hr 45 mins

Servings per Recipe: 4

Calories	355 kcal
Fat	11.9 g
Carbohydrates	47g
Protein	15.2 g
Cholesterol	19 mg
Sodium	240 mg

Ingredients

2 C. uncooked glutinous white rice

2 1/2 C. water

1 tablespoon rice vinegar

1 (6 oz.) can solid white tuna in water, drained

1 tbsp mayonnaise

1 tsp chili powder

1 tsp wasabi paste

4 sheets nori (dry seaweed)

1/2 cucumber, finely diced

1 carrot, finely diced

1 avocado - peeled, pitted and diced

Directions

1. In a pan, add the rice, water and vinegar and bring to a boil on high heat.
2. Reduce the heat to medium-low and simmer, covered for about 20-25 minutes.
3. Turn off the heat but keep the pan, covered for about 10 minutes.
4. Then keep aside to cool.
5. In a bowl, mix together the tuna, mayonnaise, chili powder and wasabi paste, breaking the tuna apart but not mashing it into a paste.
6. With a plastic wrap, cover a bamboo sushi rolling mat.
7. Place a sheet of nori, rough side up over the plastic wrap.
8. With the wet fingers, firmly pat a thick and even layer of prepared rice over the nori, covering it completely.
9. Place about 1 tablespoon each of the diced cucumber, carrot and avocado in a line along the bottom edge of the sheet.

10. Spread a line of the tuna mixture alongside the vegetables.
11. Pick up the edge of the bamboo rolling sheet, fold the bottom edge of the sheet up, enclosing the filling and tightly roll the sushi into a thick cylinder.
12. After rolling, wrap it in the mat and gently squeeze to compact it tightly.
13. Cut each roll into 6 pieces and refrigerate before serving.

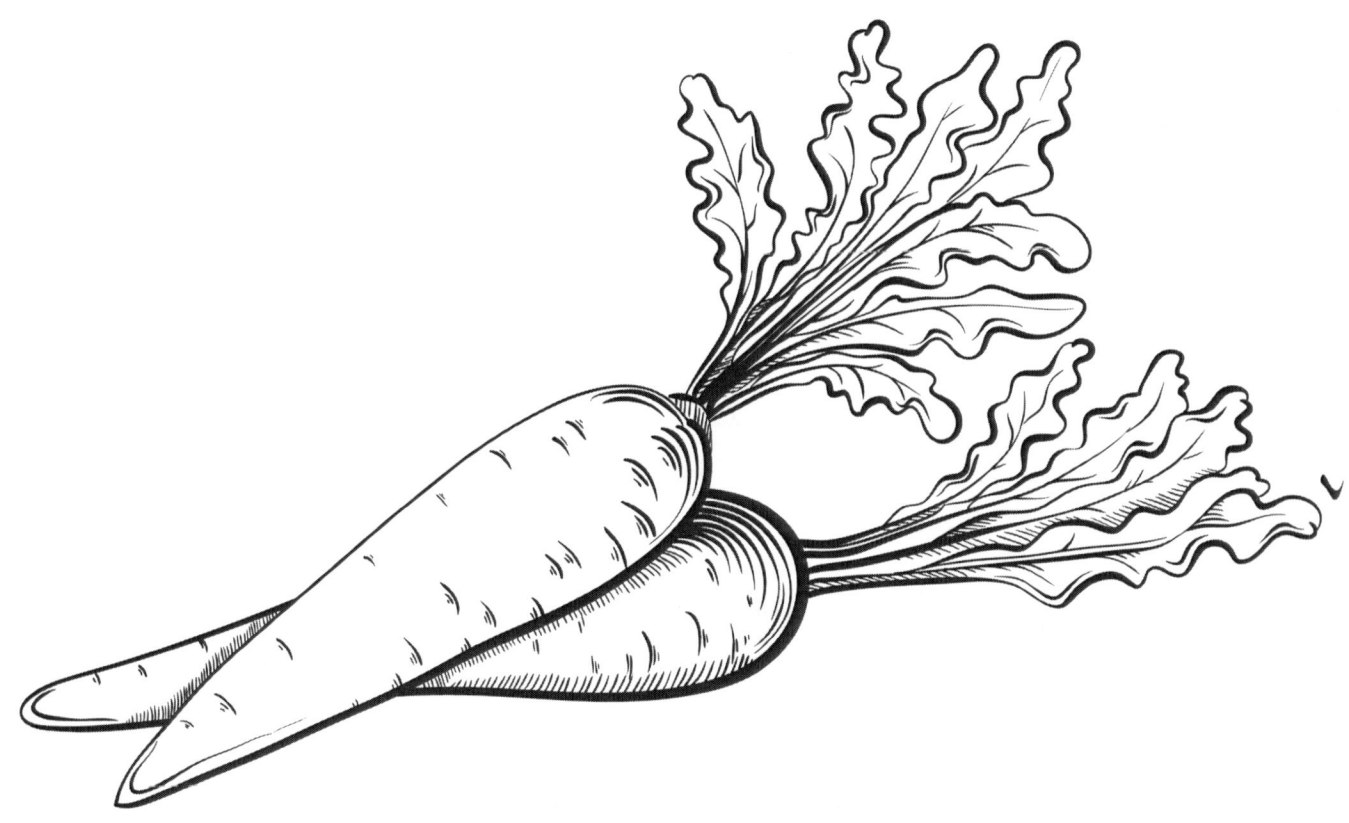

Tuna
Lunch Burritos

🥄 Prep Time: 10 mins
🕐 Total Time: 10 mins

Servings per Recipe: 4
Calories   341 kcal
Fat   12.4 g
Carbohydrates   30.2g
Protein   25.9 g
Cholesterol   29 mg
Sodium   465 mg

Ingredients

2 (6 oz.) cans tuna, drained
3 tbsp mayonnaise
1 1/2 tbsp pickle relish
1 tbsp chopped onion
1 tbsp chopped celery
1 tsp lemon juice, or to taste
1 pinch garlic salt, or to taste

4 leaves lettuce (optional)
4 (8 inch) flour tortillas, warmed

Directions

1. In a bowl, mix together the tuna, mayonnaise, pickle relish, onion, celery, lemon juice and garlic salt.
2. Arrange 1 lettuce leaf over each tortilla and place the tuna mixture in a line across the middle of each tortilla.
3. Fold opposing edges of the tortilla to overlap the filling and roll 1 of the opposing edges around the filling in a burrito-style.
4. Spread a line of the tuna mixture alongside the vegetables.
5. Pick up the edge of the bamboo rolling sheet, fold the bottom edge of the sheet up, enclosing the filling and tightly roll the sushi into a thick cylinder.
6. After rolling, wrap it in the mat and gently squeeze to compact it tightly.
7. Cut each roll into 6 pieces and refrigerate before serving.

HOMEMADE
Blackened Tuna from Baton Rouge

🥣 Prep Time: 10 mins
🕐 Total Time: 20 mins

Servings per Recipe: 6
Calories   243 kcal
Fat   14 g
Carbohydrates   1.1g
Protein   26.7 g
Cholesterol   54 mg
Sodium   546 mg

Ingredients

1 1/2 lb. fresh tuna steaks, 1 inch thick
2 tbsp Cajun seasoning
2 tbsp olive oil

2 tbsp butter

Directions

1. Coat tuna with the Cajun seasoning generously.
2. Ina large skillet, heat the oil and butter on high heat and cook the steaks in pan for 3-4 per side.

Backyard
Tuna Griller

🥄 Prep Time: 10 mins

🕐 Total Time: 1 hr 16 mins

Servings per Recipe: 4
Calories   281 kcal
Fat   11.8 g
Carbohydrates   1.8g
Protein   40 g
Cholesterol   77 mg
Sodium   644 mg

Ingredients

4 (6 oz.) albacore tuna steaks, 1 inch thick
3 tbsp extra virgin olive oil
salt and ground black pepper to taste

1 lime, juiced
1/2 C. hickory wood chips, soaked

Directions

1. In a large resealable plastic bag, place the tuna steaks and olive oil.
2. Seal and refrigerate for about 1 hour.
3. Set your grill for medium heat.
4. After the coals become very hot, spread a handful of the hickory wood chips over them for flavor.
5. Lightly, grease the grill grate.
6. Season the tuna with the salt and pepper.
7. Cook on the grill for about 3 minutes per side.
8. Transfer into a serving platter and drizzle with the fresh lime juice.
9. Serve immediately.

TUNA
California Style (Avocado and Salt)

🍲 Prep Time: 5 mins
🕐 Total Time: 5 mins

Servings per Recipe: 2
Calories   258 kcal
Fat   15.4 g
Carbohydrates   8.6g
Protein   23.4 g
Cholesterol   25 mg
Sodium   49 mg

Ingredients

1 (6 oz.) can tuna, drained
1 avocado, halved and pitted
1 pinch salt

Directions

1. In each avocado half, place half of the tuna and mix with a fork.
2. Season with the salt and serve.

Yummy
Tuna Pizza

Prep Time: 10 mins
Total Time: 30 mins

Servings per Recipe: 8
Calories	323 kcal
Fat	16.3 g
Carbohydrates	27g
Protein	18.4 g
Cholesterol	54 mg
Sodium	512 mg

Ingredients

1 (8 oz.) package cream cheese, softened
1 (14 oz.) package pre-baked pizza crust
1 (5 oz.) can tuna, drained and flaked
1/2 C. thinly sliced red onion

1 1/2 C. shredded mozzarella cheese
crushed red pepper flakes, or to taste

Directions

1. Set your oven to 400 degrees F before doing anything else.
2. Spread the softened cream cheese over the pre-baked crust and top with the tuna and onions.
3. Sprinkle with the shredded mozzarella cheese and red pepper flakes.
4. Cook in the oven for about 15-20 minutes.

TUNA
Cheese Burgers

Prep Time: 15 mins
Total Time: 30 mins

Servings per Recipe: 4
Calories	427 kcal
Fat	21.9 g
Carbohydrates	31.2g
Protein	25.3 g
Cholesterol	180 mg
Sodium	1045 mg

Ingredients

3 eggs
1/4 lb. processed cheese food, diced
2 tbsp sweet pickle relish
1 (6 oz.) can tuna, drained
2 tbsp minced onion

1/2 C. creamy salad dressing, e.g. Miracle Whip (TM)
3 tbsp chopped stuffed green olives
4 hamburger buns

Directions

1. Set your oven to 400 degrees F before doing anything else.
2. In a pan of cold water, add the eggs. Bring to a boil and immediately remove from the heat.
3. Keep aside the eggs, covered in hot water for about 10-12 minutes.
4. Remove from the hot water and keep aside to cool.
5. Peel the eggs and then chop.
6. In a large bowl, add the eggs, processed cheese food, sweet pickle relish, tuna, onion, creamy salad dressing and green olives and mix completely.
7. Spread the mixture over the hamburger buns and wrap in foil paper.
8. Cook in the oven for about 15 minutes.

Mediterranean
Salad

Prep Time: 15 mins
Total Time: 15 mins

Servings per Recipe: 8
Calories   362 kcal
Fat   19.5 g
Carbohydrates   27.1g
Protein   18.9 g
Cholesterol   119 mg
Sodium   554 mg

Ingredients

1 (6 oz.) can tuna, drained
1 (15 oz.) can chickpeas (garbanzo beans), drained
2 hard-boiled eggs, chopped
1 cucumber, peeled and diced

1 head iceberg lettuce, torn into bite-sized pieces
1/2 C. French dressing

Directions

1. In a large bowl, add the tuna, chickpeas, chopped hard-boiled eggs, diced cucumber, iceberg lettuce and French dressing and toss to coat well.

FANCY
Tuna Appetizer

Prep Time: 15 mins
Total Time: 15 mins

Servings per Recipe: 24

Calories	65 kcal
Fat	5.8 g
Carbohydrates	0.9g
Protein	2.8 g
Cholesterol	12 mg
Sodium	31 mg

Ingredients

1 (6 oz.) can tuna, drained and flaked
1 (8 oz.) package cream cheese, softened
3/4 C. chopped pecans

1/4 C. chopped onion

Directions

1. In a medium bowl, add the tuna, cream cheese, 1/2 of the pecans and onion and mix till well combined.
2. Make a loaf from the mixture and coat with the remaining pecans.
3. Refrigerate till serving.

Delicious
Tuna Spread

Prep Time: 5 mins
Total Time: 5 mins

Servings per Recipe: 8	
Calories	46 kcal
Fat	3 g
Carbohydrates	0.6g
Protein	4.2 g
Cholesterol	6 mg
Sodium	72 mg

Ingredients

1 (5 oz.) can chunk light tuna in water, drained and flaked
2 tbsp mayonnaise
1 tbsp prepared yellow mustard
1 1/2 tsp creamy prepared horseradish

1 tsp lemon juice
1 tsp garlic powder
1 pinch salt

Directions

1. In a bowl, add the tuna, mayonnaise, yellow mustard, horseradish, lemon juice, garlic powder and salt and mix till well combined.

CREAM
of Tuna

🍲 Prep Time: 10 mins

🕐 Total Time: 25 mins

Servings per Recipe: 6	
Calories	201 kcal
Fat	11.6 g
Carbohydrates	7.4g
Protein	16.7 g
Cholesterol	39 mg
Sodium	433 mg

Ingredients

1/4 C. butter
1/2 C. frozen peas
1 small onion, chopped
1 clove garlic, minced
1 (10.75 oz.) can condensed cream of mushroom soup

1/2 C. milk, or as needed
2 (6 oz.) cans tuna, drained
salt and ground black pepper to taste

Directions

1. In a pan, melt the butter on medium heat and sauté the peas, onion and garlic for about 5-7 minutes.
2. Place the mushroom soup over the peas mixture and add enough milk to the mixture to thicken the soup.
3. With a fork, flake the tuna and add into the skillet.
4. Season with the salt and pepper and cook for about 10 minutes.

Italian
Tuna Loaf

🥄 Prep Time: 15 mins
🕐 Total Time: 40 mins

Servings per Recipe: 6
Calories   273 kcal
Fat   7.7 g
Carbohydrates   29.2g
Protein   20.6 g
Cholesterol   54 mg
Sodium   712 mg

Ingredients

2 (6 oz.) cans solid white tuna packed in water, drained
1 (10.75 oz.) can condensed cream of chicken soup
1/2 (10.75 oz.) can milk
1 (4 oz.) packet saltine crackers, crushed

3 slices white bread, crumbled into fine crumbs
1/2 onion, finely chopped
1 large egg
ground black pepper to taste

Directions

1. Set your oven to 350 degrees F before doing anything else and lightly, grease a large loaf pan.
2. In a bowl, add the tuna, cream of chicken soup, milk, cracker crumbs, bread crumbs, onion, egg and black pepper and mix till well combined.
3. Transfer the mixture into the prepared loaf pan and with a spatula, smooth the top surface.
4. Cook in the oven for about 25-30 minutes or till a toothpick inserted into the loaf comes out clean.

EASY HOMEMADE
Tuna Mousse

🥣 Prep Time: 20 mins
🕐 Total Time: 8 hrs 20 mins

Servings per Recipe: 20
Calories   153 kcal
Fat   13.7 g
Carbohydrates   2g
Protein   5.8 g
Cholesterol   21 mg
Sodium   426 mg

Ingredients

2 envelopes unflavored gelatin
1/2 C. water
1 (10.75 oz.) can condensed cream of mushroom soup
1 (8 oz.) package cream cheese, softened
1 1/2 tbsp Worcestershire sauce
1 C. mayonnaise
salt and pepper to taste

1 tsp onion salt
1 tsp celery salt (optional)
1 (12.5 oz.) can water-packed tuna, drained

Directions

1. Line a pie pan with the plastic wrap.
2. In a small bowl, add the gelatin and water and stir to dissolve, then keep aside.
3. In a large pan, heat the soup and cream cheese till soft and smooth.
4. Remove the pan from the heat.
5. In the pan, add the gelatin mixture, Worcestershire sauce, mayonnaise, salt, pepper, onion salt, celery salt and tuna fish and stir till smooth.
6. Transfer the mixture into the prepared pie pan and refrigerate, covered to chill for overnight. Just before serving, remove the tuna mousse from the pie pan and serve.

Mac and Cheese
Tuna Quick Throw-Together Dinner

Prep Time: 10 mins
Total Time: 50 mins

Servings per Recipe: 4
Calories	459 kcal
Fat	15.3 g
Carbohydrates	56.3g
Protein	23.8 g
Cholesterol	21 mg
Sodium	908 mg

Ingredients

6 C. water
1 (7.25 oz.) package macaroni and cheese dinner mix
1/4 C. margarine, cut into pieces
1/4 C. milk
1 (6 oz.) can tuna, drained and flaked
1 (4.5 oz.) can sliced mushrooms, drained
1 C. bread crumbs

Directions

1. Set your oven to 350 degrees F before doing anything else.
2. In a large pan of lightly salted boiling water, cook the macaroni for about 7 - 8 minutes, stirring occasionally.
3. Drain well.
4. In the same pan, return the macaroni.
5. Add the cheese sauce mixture from the packet, margarine and milk and stir till the margarine melts and the macaroni is evenly coated with the sauce.
6. Add the tuna and mushrooms and stir to combine.
7. Transfer the macaroni mixture into a small casserole dish and sprinkle with the bread crumbs evenly.
8. Cook in the oven for about 30 minutes.

A SIMPLE
Tuna Snack

Prep Time: 30 mins
Total Time: 1 hr

Servings per Recipe: 12

Calories	163 kcal
Fat	9.7 g
Carbohydrates	12.6g
Protein	6.1 g
Cholesterol	36 mg
Sodium	243 mg

Ingredients

1 1/2 C. water
3/4 C. uncooked long-grain white rice
1 tbsp vegetable oil
1 medium onion, diced
1 (6 oz.) can water packed tuna, drained and flaked
1/2 C. milk
3 tbsp self-rising flour
1 tbsp chopped fresh parsley

1 tsp white sugar
1 tsp white vinegar
1 tsp salt
1 tsp ground black pepper
2 large eggs
1 quart vegetable oil for frying

Directions

1. In a pan of boiling water, stir in the rice.
2. Reduce the heat and simmer, covered for about 20 minutes.
3. In a small pan, heat 1 tbsp of the oil on low heat and stir in the onion.
4. Cook, covered for about 5 minutes.
5. In a large bowl, mix together the tuna, milk, flour, parsley, sugar, vinegar, salt, pepper, rice, onion, and eggs.
6. Make about 12 balls from the mixture.
7. In a large, heavy skillet, heat 1 quart oil and fry the tuna balls in batches till golden brown.
8. Transfer the balls onto paper towels lines plate to drain.

Tuna
and Onions

Prep Time: 5 mins
Total Time: 15 mins

Servings per Recipe: 1

Calories	260 kcal
Fat	1.6 g
Carbohydrates	14.9 g
Protein	45 g
Cholesterol	50 mg
Sodium	89 mg

Ingredients

1 (6 oz.) can tuna
1/3 C. water
1 tsp onion powder

1 tsp garlic powder
1 onion, sliced into rings

Directions

1. In a medium pan, add the tuna and place the water over it.
2. Sprinkle with the onion powder and garlic powder and arrange the onion rings on top.
3. Simmer, covered for about 5 minutes.

SATISFYING
Tuna Sandwich

Prep Time: 5 mins

Total Time: 30 mins

Servings per Recipe: 3

Calories	333 kcal
Fat	11.9 g
Carbohydrates	32g
Protein	24.5 g
Cholesterol	158 mg
Sodium	994 mg

Ingredients

1 (10.75 oz.) can condensed cream of mushroom soup

2 hard-cooked eggs, sliced

1 (6 oz.) can tuna, drained

6 slices whole wheat bread

Directions

1. Prepare the cream of mushroom soup according to the directions on the can.
2. Stir in the canned tuna and egg slices and cook till heated completely.
3. Meanwhile, toast the bread slices.
4. Spread the tuna mixture over the toasted slices and serve.

Thursday's
Tuna

🥄 Prep Time: 20 mins
🕐 Total Time: 40 mins

Servings per Recipe: 6

Calories	551 kcal
Fat	24.7 g
Carbohydrates	40g
Protein	41.8 g
Cholesterol	182 mg
Sodium	418 mg

Ingredients

1/4 C. butter
2 tbsp all-purpose flour
2 C. milk
1/2 tsp dry mustard
1 C. shredded Cheddar cheese
salt and pepper to taste
3 (7 oz.) cans tuna packed in water, drained

3 tbsp chopped fresh parsley
3 hard-cooked eggs, peeled and chopped
1 C. crushed plain potato chips
1 pinch paprika, for garnish
8 oz. fettuccini pasta

Directions

1. Set your oven to 350 degrees F before doing anything else.
2. In a small skillet, melt the butter on low heat and stir in the flour till smooth.
3. Cook, stirring continuously for about 1 minute.
4. Remove the pan from the heat and slowly, stir in the milk till smooth.
5. Return the pan to heat and cook, stirring continuously for about 3 minutes.
6. Remove from the heat and add the mustard powder and a little more than half of the Cheddar cheese and beat till melted. Season with the salt and pepper.
7. With a fork, flake the tuna and stir it into the sauce with the parsley and chopped egg.
8. Transfer the mixture into a 9-inch round cake pan.
9. In a bowl, mix together the potato chips and remaining Cheddar cheese.
10. Top the tuna mixture with the potato chips mixture evenly and lightly, sprinkle with the paprika.
11. Cook in the oven for about 20 minutes.

12. Meanwhile in a large pan of lightly salted boiling water, cook the fettuccini pasta for about 8 minutes.
13. Drain well.
14. Serve the tuna mixture over the fettucine.

Creamy
Broccoli Dumplings

Prep Time: 10 mins
Total Time: 40 mins

Servings per Recipe: 6
Calories	341 kcal
Fat	16.6 g
Carbohydrates	27.8g
Protein	19.4 g
Cholesterol	88 mg
Sodium	929 mg

Ingredients

1 (6 oz.) can tuna, drained
1 egg
1 tsp dried parsley
1/2 C. shredded Cheddar cheese
1/2 tsp salt
1/2 tsp ground black pepper
1 (10.75 oz.) can condensed cream of broccoli soup

1 (12 fluid oz.) can evaporated milk
2 tsp chopped pimento
1 (8 oz.) package refrigerated crescent rolls

Directions

1. Set your oven to 375 degrees F before doing anything else.
2. In a bowl, mix together the tuna, egg, parsley, cheese, salt and pepper.
3. In another bowl, mix together the soup, milk, and pimentos together.
4. Flatten the crescent rolls one at a time and place a small amount of the tuna mixture over each roll.
5. Fold over and seal the edges.
6. Arrange the stuffed crescent rolls in a baking dish and top with the soup and milk mixture evenly.
7. Cook in the oven for about 30 minutes.

HOW TO MAKE
a Tuna Melt

Prep Time: 15 mins

Total Time: 25 mins

Servings per Recipe: 8

Calories	483 kcal
Fat	27.7 g
Carbohydrates	34.1g
Protein	24.5 g
Cholesterol	41 mg
Sodium	716 mg

Ingredients

1 (1 lb.) loaf French bread
1 small sweet onion, peeled and diced
1 (12 oz.) can tuna, drained

2 C. mozzarella cheese, shredded
1 C. mayonnaise

Directions

1. Set your oven to 350 degrees F before doing anything else.
2. In a bowl, add the sweet onion, drained tuna, mozzarella and mayonnaise and mix till well combined.
3. Spread the tuna mixture over the French bread slices to form a sandwich.
4. Arrange the sandwiches onto a cookie sheet.
5. Cook in the oven for about 10 minutes.

Milanese
Tuna

🥄 Prep Time: 20 mins
🕐 Total Time: 1 hr

Servings per Recipe: 6
Calories	607 kcal
Fat	25.4 g
Carbohydrates	69.6g
Protein	27.5 g
Cholesterol	35 mg
Sodium	853 mg

Ingredients

3 tbsp olive oil
1 clove garlic, sliced
1 white onion, diced
1 C. water
2 (6 oz.) cans tuna in olive oil
1 (6 oz.) can pitted black olives, drained and chopped
1 (15 oz.) can garbanzo beans, drained and rinsed

1/2 tsp garlic salt
1/2 tsp ground black pepper
1 lb. penne pasta
1/4 C. grated Romano cheese

Directions

1. In a large pan, heat the olive oil on medium heat and sauté the garlic till golden.
2. Stir in onion and water and cook till onion becomes tender.
3. Stir in the tuna with its oil, olives, beans, garlic salt and pepper and reduce the heat to medium-low.
4. Simmer, covered while pasta is cooking.
5. In a large pan of lightly salted boiling water, cook the egg noodles for about 8-10 minutes.
6. Drain well.
7. Add the pasta into the tuna mixture and toss to coat well.
8. Top with the Romano cheese and serve.

SIMPLEST
Tuna Cheddar French Onion Bake

Prep Time: 15 mins

Total Time: 45 mins

Servings per Recipe: 8
Calories	469 kcal
Fat	28.5 g
Carbohydrates	37.1g
Protein	12.8 g
Cholesterol	24 mg
Sodium	708 mg

Ingredients

3 C. cooked macaroni
1 (6 oz.) can tuna, drained
1 (10.75 oz.) can condensed cream of chicken soup

1 C. shredded Cheddar cheese
1 1/2 C. French fried onions

Directions

1. Set your oven to 350 degrees F before doing anything else.
2. In a 9x13-inch baking dish, add the macaroni, tuna and soup and mix till well combined.
3. Sprinkle with the cheese.
4. Cook in the oven for about 25 minutes.
5. Top with the fried onions and cook in the oven for about 5 minutes.
6. Serve hot.

6 Ingredient
Tuna Dinner

Prep Time: 20 mins
Total Time: 35 mins

Servings per Recipe: 4

Calories	470 kcal
Fat	23.1 g
Carbohydrates	45.6g
Protein	20.5 g
Cholesterol	78 mg
Sodium	551 mg

Ingredients

1 (8 oz.) package egg noodles
1 tbsp vegetable oil
1 onion, chopped
1 (6 oz.) can tuna, drained

1 (10.75 oz.) can condensed cream of mushroom soup
1 (8 oz.) container sour cream

Directions

1. In a large pan of lightly salted boiling water, cook the egg noodles for about 8-10 minutes.
2. Drain well.
3. In a large skillet, heat the oil on medium heat and sauté the onion till browned.
4. Stir in the tuna, mushroom soup and sour cream and cook till heated completely.
5. Stir in the cooked egg noodles and serve.

TUNA
Steaks 101

Prep Time: 10 mins
Total Time: 51 mins

Servings per Recipe: 4	
Calories	200 kcal
Fat	7.9 g
Carbohydrates	3.7g
Protein	27.4 g
Cholesterol	51 mg
Sodium	945 mg

Ingredients

1/4 C. orange juice
1/4 C. soy sauce
2 tbsp olive oil
1 tbsp lemon juice
2 tbsp chopped fresh parsley

1 clove garlic, minced
1/2 tsp chopped fresh oregano
1/2 tsp ground black pepper
4 (4 oz.) tuna steaks

Directions

1. In a large non-reactive dish, add the orange juice, soy sauce, olive oil, lemon juice, parsley, garlic, oregano and pepper and mix till well combined.
2. Add the tuna steaks and coat with the mixture generously.
3. Refrigerate, covered for at least 30 minutes.
4. Set your grill for high heat and lightly, grease the grill grate.
5. Cook the tuna steaks on grill for about 5-6 minutes.
6. Flip the steaks and coat with the marinade.
7. Cook on the grill for about 5 minutes.

Shibuya
Terminal Tuna

Prep Time: 5 mins
Total Time: 45 mins

Servings per Recipe: 4
Calories	551 kcal
Fat	41.6 g
Carbohydrates	12.9 g
Protein	30.7 g
Cholesterol	51 mg
Sodium	2803 mg

Ingredients

1 C. teriyaki sauce
3/4 C. olive oil
2 tbsp minced garlic
1 tsp ground black pepper

4 (4 oz.) fillets yellowfin tuna

Directions

1. In a large resealable plastic bag, mix together the teriyaki sauce, oil, garlic and pepper.
2. Add the tuna fillets and seal the bag with as little air in it as possible.
3. Shake well to coat the tuna fillets with marinade.
4. Refrigerate to marinade for about 30 minutes.
5. Set your outdoor grill for high heat and lightly, grease the grill grate.
6. Remove the tuna from marinade.
7. Cook the tuna fillets on grill for about 3-5 minutes per side.

PEPPERY
Cayenne Tuna

🥣 Prep Time: 5 mins

🕐 Total Time: 17 mins

Servings per Recipe: 2

Calories	301 kcal
Fat	17.8 g
Carbohydrates	0.7g
Protein	33.3 g
Cholesterol	71 mg
Sodium	1034 mg

Ingredients

2 (5 oz.) ahi tuna steaks
1 tsp kosher salt
1/4 tsp cayenne pepper
1/2 tbsp butter

2 tbsp olive oil
1 tsp whole peppercorns

Directions

1. Season the tuna steaks with the salt and cayenne pepper.
2. In a skillet, heat the olive oil and butter on medium-high heat and cook the peppercorns for about 5 minutes.
3. Gently place the seasoned tuna in the skillet and cook for about 1 1/2 minutes per side.

Barcelona
Tuna Appetizer

Prep Time: 20 mins
Total Time: 20 mins

Servings per Recipe: 4	
Calories	294 kcal
Fat	18.2 g
Carbohydrates	11g
Protein	23.9 g
Cholesterol	27 mg
Sodium	154 mg

Ingredients

1 (12 oz.) can solid white tuna packed in water, drained
1 tbsp mayonnaise
3 green onions, thinly sliced, plus additional for garnish
1/2 red bell pepper, chopped

1 dash balsamic vinegar
black pepper to taste
1 pinch garlic salt, or to taste
2 ripe avocados, halved and pitted

Directions

1. In a bowl, mix together the tuna, mayonnaise, green onions, red pepper, balsamic vinegar, pepper and garlic salt.
2. Stuff the avocado halves with the tuna mixture evenly.
3. Sprinkle with a dash of black pepper and serve with a garnishing of the reserved green onions.

Tuna Salad

Prep Time: 10 mins
Total Time: 1 hr 10 mins

Servings per Recipe: 2
Calories   432 kcal
Fat   31 g
Carbohydrates   12.8g
Protein   27.2 g
Cholesterol   141 mg
Sodium   517 mg

Ingredients

1 (6 oz.) can chunk light tuna, drained
1/4 C. creamy salad dressing (such as Miracle Whip(R))
1 hard-boiled egg, chopped

1/2 apple, diced
1/2 C. chopped toasted pecans
salt and pepper to taste

Directions

1. In a large bowl, add all the ingredients and stir to combine.
2. Refrigerate to chill for at least 1 hour before serving.

Apple
and Tuna Lunch Box

Prep Time: 15 mins
Total Time: 15 mins

Servings per Recipe: 2
Calories	267 kcal
Fat	2.6 g
Carbohydrates	30g
Protein	29 g
Cholesterol	25 mg
Sodium	803 mg

Ingredients

1 (6 oz.) can tuna in water, drained
1/4 C. sauerkraut
1/4 C. finely chopped apple
2 tbsp Dijon mustard

1 tbsp balsamic vinegar
4 slices whole wheat bread, toasted

Directions

1. In a large bowl, add all the ingredients and stir to combine.
2. Spread over the toasted wheat bread slices and serve.

RECESSION
Special Tuna

Prep Time: 5 mins
Total Time: 15 mins

Servings per Recipe: 4
Calories   226 kcal
Fat   8.8 g
Carbohydrates   19.9g
Protein   16.1 g
Cholesterol   35 mg
Sodium   367 mg

Ingredients

2 tbsp butter
2 tbsp all-purpose flour
1 1/2 C. milk
1 (6 oz.) can chunk light tuna in water, drained and
flaked

salt and ground black pepper to taste
4 slices bread, toasted

Directions

1. In a small pan, melt the butter on medium heat and stir in the flour till smooth.
2. Slowly, add the milk, beating continuously and bring to a simmer.
3. Cook for about 5 minutes.
4. Reduce the heat to medium-low and stir in the tuna, salt and pepper.
5. Cook for about 2-3 minutes.
6. Spread the tuna mixture over the toasted bread slices and serve.

How to Make
Tuna

🍳 Prep Time: 15 mins
🕐 Total Time: 20 mins

Servings per Recipe: 2
Calories   367 kcal
Fat   29.3 g
Carbohydrates   2.4g
Protein   24.2 g
Cholesterol   147 mg
Sodium   284 mg

Ingredients

1 (5 oz.) can tuna packed in water, drained
1 egg
1/2 stalk celery, chopped
2 tbsp mayonnaise
2 tbsp chopped walnuts
2 tbsp chopped fresh parsley

1 tsp chopped fresh dill
1 tbsp butter
1/4 C. shredded Cheddar cheese

Directions

1. In a bowl, add the tuna, egg, celery, mayonnaise, walnuts, parsley and dill and mix till well combined.
2. Make 2 equal sized patties from the mixture.
3. In a skillet, melt the butter on medium heat and cook the patties for about 2-3 minutes.
4. Flip the patties and top each with the Cheddar cheese.
5. Cook for about 2-3 minutes more.

GOURMET
Tuna

Prep Time: 15 mins
Total Time: 25 mins

Servings per Recipe: 4

Calories	263 kcal
Fat	10.8 g
Carbohydrates	13.6g
Protein	26.9 g
Cholesterol	118 mg
Sodium	207 mg

Ingredients

2 (6 oz.) cans tuna, drained
2 eggs
1/2 C. bread crumbs
1/2 C. chopped onion
1/2 C. chopped celery
1 1/2 tbsp prepared horseradish

1 tbsp lemon juice
1 clove garlic, minced
1/4 tsp ground black pepper
2 tbsp vegetable oil

Directions

1. In a bowl, add the tuna, eggs, bread crumbs, onion, celery, horseradish, lemon juice, garlic and black pepper and mix till well combined.
2. Make 4 equal sized patties from the mixture.
3. In a skillet, heat the oil on medium heat and cook the patties for about 5 minutes from both sides.

Tuna
and Potatoes

Prep Time: 20 mins
Total Time: 20 mins

Servings per Recipe: 5
Calories	435 kcal
Fat	35.8 g
Carbohydrates	17.9g
Protein	10.3 g
Cholesterol	23 mg
Sodium	331 mg

Ingredients

1 (6 oz.) can tuna, drained
1 C. shredded carrot
1 C. diced celery
1/4 C. minced onion

3/4 C. mayonnaise
1/2 (9 oz.) can shoestring potatoes

Directions

1. In a bowl, break the tuna in pieces.
2. Add the carrot, celery, onion and mayonnaise and stir to combine.
3. While serving, fold in the shoestring potatoes.

PEPPER
and Coconut Tuna

🥣 Prep Time: 20 mins
🕐 Total Time: 20 mins

Servings per Recipe: 4	
Calories	120 kcal
Fat	5.6 g
Carbohydrates	3.5g
Protein	14.4 g
Cholesterol	26 mg
Sodium	148 mg

Ingredients

8 oz. ice-cold sushi-grade yellowfin tuna steak, diced
1/4 C. coconut milk
2 tbsp chopped cashews
2 tbsp sliced red onion
1 tbsp minced serrano pepper
1 tbsp torn cilantro leaves

2 tsp grated fresh ginger
salt to taste
1 lime, juiced
1 pinch red pepper flakes

Directions

1. In a bowl, add the tuna, 1/2 of the coconut milk, cashews, red onion, Serrano pepper, cilantro, ginger, salt and lime juice and stir till well combined.
2. Drizzle in the remaining coconut milk till desired consistency is achieved.
3. Transfer the tartare into a bowl and serve with a sprinkling of the red pepper flakes.

Tuna
Breakfast

🥣 Prep Time: 10 mins
🕐 Total Time: 15 mins

Servings per Recipe: 1
Calories	833 kcal
Fat	47.1 g
Carbohydrates	33.2g
Protein	66.3 g
Cholesterol	133 mg
Sodium	1098 mg

Ingredients

1 (6 oz.) can chunk light tuna, drained
2 tbsp mayonnaise
1 tsp Dijon mustard
1 bagel, split and toasted

1/2 C. shredded Cheddar cheese

Directions

1. Set your oven to 300 degrees F before doing anything else.
2. In a bowl, add the tuna, mayonnaise and mustard and with a fork, mash till well combined.
3. Spread tuna mixture over each bagel half evenly and sprinkle with the shredded Cheddar cheese.
4. Arrange the bagel halves onto a baking sheet.
5. Cook in the oven for about 5 minutes.

MEXICO CITY
Sandwich

🥣 Prep Time: 30 mins
🕐 Total Time: 30 mins

Servings per Recipe: 5	
Calories	477 kcal
Fat	19.3 g
Carbohydrates	52.3g
Protein	24 g
Cholesterol	26 mg
Sodium	1090 mg

Ingredients

1 (1 lb.) loaf French bread
10 oz. ahi (yellowfin) tuna, sushi-grade - sliced 1 inch long and 1/8 inch thick
1/4 C. onion, cut into 1/8-inch dice
2 tbsp capers, drained
3 oz. olive oil

3 tbsp fresh lemon juice
1 tsp kosher salt
1/4 tsp freshly ground black pepper

Directions

1. Cut the French bread into 1/4 inch thick slices and keep aside.
2. In a flat nonreactive dish, arrange the tuna slices in a single layer and top with the onion and capers.
3. Drizzle with the olive oil and lemon juice and sprinkle with the kosher salt and black pepper.
4. Serve tuna slices over French bread slices.

Cheddar
Maple and Onion Tuna

🥣 Prep Time: 10 mins
🕐 Total Time: 25 mins

Servings per Recipe: 4
Calories	649 kcal
Fat	30.1 g
Carbohydrates	49.3g
Protein	43.3 g
Cholesterol	102 mg
Sodium	1088 mg

Ingredients

2 tbsp butter
1/2 large sweet red onion, thinly sliced
1 tbsp maple syrup
2 (6 oz.) cans tuna, drained
2 tbsp creamy salad dressing (such as Miracle Whip(R))

salt and ground black pepper to taste
1 (12 oz.) loaf Italian olive bread
8 oz. shredded Cheddar cheese

Directions

1. In a small frying pan, melt the butter on medium heat and sauté the onion for about 3 minutes.
2. Reduce the heat to medium-low and stir in the maple syrup.
3. Cook for about 7-10 minutes.
4. Set your oven to the broiler and arrange oven rack about 8-inches from the heating element.
5. In a bowl, mix together the tuna, salad dressing, salt and pepper.
6. Slice the bread loaf in half horizontally, then halve both pieces lengthwise, making four equal pieces.
7. Arrange the bread pieces, crust-side down onto a baking sheet.
8. Place the tuna mixture over bread pieces, followed by the onion and Cheddar cheese evenly.
9. Cook under the broiler for about 5 minutes.

SIMPLY THYME
and Tuna with Sea Salt

🍲 Prep Time: 10 mins
🕐 Total Time: 1 d 1 h 20 m

Servings per Recipe: 2
Calories   608 kcal
Fat   36 g
Carbohydrates   1.3g
Protein   66.5 g
Cholesterol   109 mg
Sodium   271 mg

Ingredients

2 (10 oz.) thick-cut ahi tuna steaks
2 cloves garlic, bruised
6 sprigs fresh thyme
1 pinch red pepper flakes

2 C. olive oil
sea salt to taste

Directions

1. Keep the tuna in room temperature for about 10-15 minutes.
2. In a heavy skillet, place the garlic, thyme, and red pepper flakes and pour the olive oil on top.
3. Cook on medium heat for about 5-10 minutes.
4. Gently, place the tuna in hot oil and reduce the heat to low.
5. Cook for about 5-7 minutes, spooning oil over the top of the steaks continuously.
6. Remove from the heat and arrange the steaks into a baking dish.
7. Place the hot oil and herbs over the steaks and keep aside to in the room temperature.
8. With a plastic wrap, cover the baking dish tightly and refrigerate for about 24 hours.
9. Remove the tuna steaks from the oil and serve with a sprinkling of the sea salt.

Smoky
Tuna

Prep Time: 5 mins
Total Time: 31 mins

Servings per Recipe: 2
Calories	287 kcal
Fat	4.7 g
Carbohydrates	4.3g
Protein	54.4 g
Cholesterol	102 mg
Sodium	1000 mg

Ingredients

2 (8 oz.) fresh tuna steaks
1 tsp vegetable oil
2 tbsp soy sauce
2 tbsp seasoned rice vinegar
1 tbsp finely grated raw horseradish root
4 cherry tomatoes, sliced

1/2 tsp hot chili paste (such as sambal oelek)
1 tbsp minced green onion

Directions

1. Set your outdoor grill for medium-high heat and lightly, grease the grill grate.
2. Coat the tuna steaks with vegetable oil lightly.
3. In a bowl, add the soy sauce, rice vinegar, horseradish, cherry tomatoes and hot chili paste and mix till well combined.
4. Keep aside for about 20 minutes.
5. Arrange the tuna steaks over the hottest part of the grill and cook for about 3 minutes from both sides.
6. In a serving plate, place the steaks and pour the soy sauce mixture on top.
7. Serve with a garnishing of the green onion.

PARTY-TIME
Tuna

Prep Time: 30 mins

Total Time: 40 mins

Servings per Recipe: 12	
Calories	153 kcal
Fat	8.1 g
Carbohydrates	11.8g
Protein	7.2 g
Cholesterol	11 mg
Sodium	249 mg

Ingredients

1/3 C. gyoza dipping sauce
2 tsp granulated sugar
1 clove garlic, minced
1/2 tsp sesame oil
1/4 tsp crushed red pepper flakes
1 sheet frozen puff pastry, thawed
1 tbsp all-purpose flour
2 (5 oz.) cans Bumble Bee(R) Solid White Albacore
Tuna in Water, drained

1/3 C. finely diced fresh mango
1 tbsp chopped green onion
2 tbsp minced green bell pepper
1/2 tbsp toasted sesame seeds (optional)

Directions

1. Set your oven to 400 degrees F before doing anything else.
2. In a small pan, mix together the gyoza dipping sauce, sugar, garlic, toasted sesame oil and red pepper flakes on medium heat and cook till the mixture reduces to half.
3. Remove from the heat and keep aside.
4. Place the defrosted puff pastry sheet onto a lightly floured smooth surface.
5. Dust the top of the puff pastry sheet with the flour and roll into an 11 x 13-inch rectangle.
6. Cut the pastry sheet into 24 equal size rectangles by cutting the 11-inch dimension into 4 equal strips, and then cutting the 13-inch dimension into 6 equal strips.
7. Arrange each rectangle over the hole of a mini muffin cup and push the middle of the dough down into the muffin cup to form a cup.

8. Cook in the oven for about 8 minutes.
9. Remove from the oven and with a fork, punch down the puffed up middle portion of the pastry cup.
10. Cook in the oven for about 3 minutes.
11. Remove from the oven and with a fork, punch down the centers again, forming a nice hole for the filling.
12. Keep aside to cool completely before removing from the muffin tin.
13. In a medium bowl, add the tuna, mango and sweet bell pepper and gently, toss to combine.
14. With a small spoon, fill each puff pastry cup with the tuna filling and drizzle the reserved sauce on top.
15. Serve with a garnishing of the chopped green onions and toasted sesame seeds.

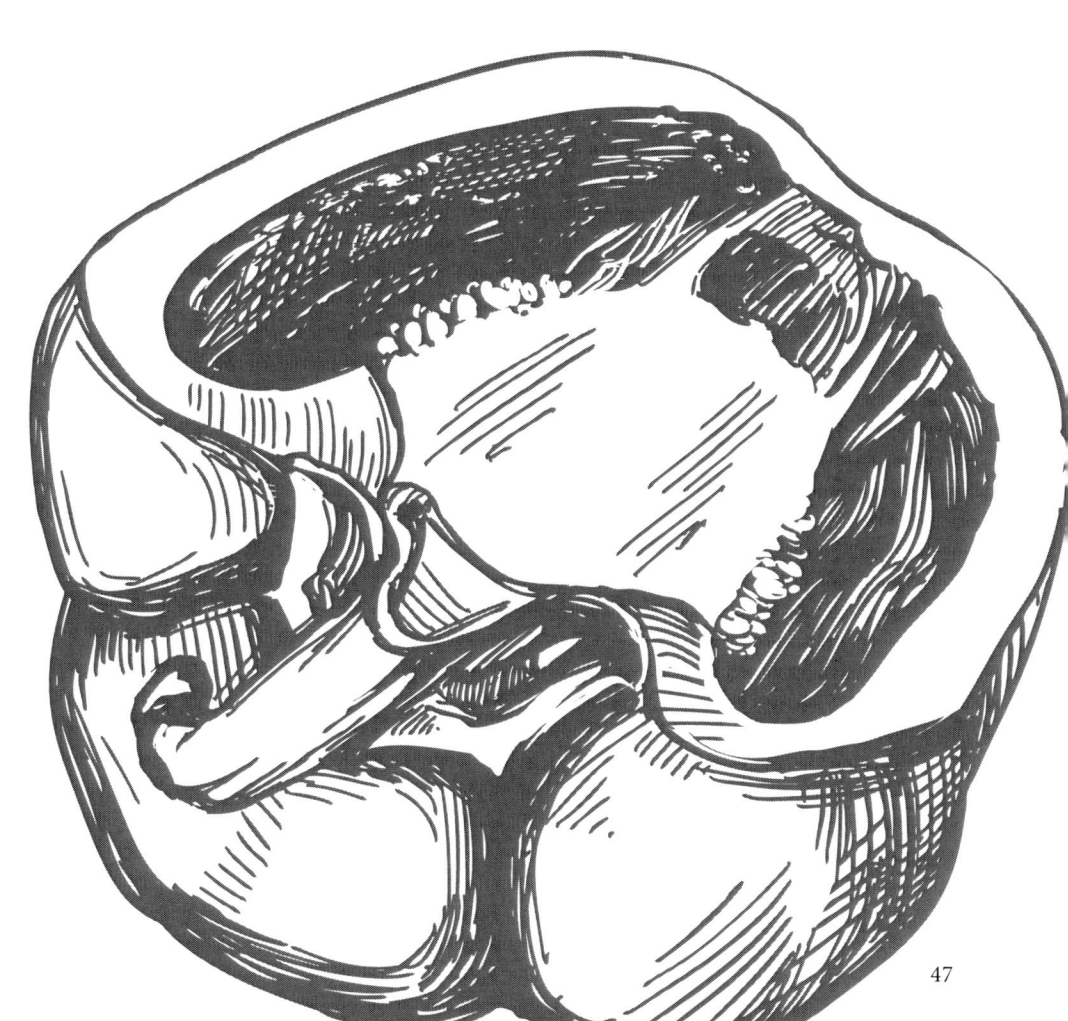

ALL AMERICAN
Omelet

Prep Time: 10 mins
Total Time: 20 mins

Servings per Recipe: 2
Calories	477 kcal
Fat	12.3 g
Carbohydrates	52.3g
Protein	22 g
Cholesterol	26 mg
Sodium	690 mg

Ingredients

2 tsp vegetable oil
1/2 small onion, chopped
1 (6 oz.) can tuna, drained
1/3 C. sour cream
3 tbsp cream cheese
1/2 C. shredded mozzarella cheese
1 (2.25 oz.) can sliced black olives

1/8 tsp dried dill weed
1/8 tsp garlic powder
5 eggs
1/4 C. milk
2 tsp vegetable oil

Directions

1. In a large skillet, heat 2 tsp of the vegetable oil on medium heat and sauté the onion till the onion just begins to brown.
2. In a large bowl, add the tuna, sour cream, cream cheese, mozzarella cheese, olives, dill, garlic powder and cooked onion and mix well.
3. In another large bowl, add the eggs and milk and beat.
4. In the same skillet used to cook the onion, heat 2 tsp of the oil and place the egg mixture.
5. As eggs set, lift the edges to let the liquid to run underneath evenly.
6. After the eggs are almost set, place the tuna mixture over one half of the eggs and fold the other half over the filling.
7. Cover the skillet and immediately, remove from the heat.
8. Keep the skillet, covered till the cheese melts.

Monday's
Pita Sandwich

Prep Time: 10 mins
Total Time: 15 mins

Servings per Recipe: 1

Calories	394 kcal
Fat	21.6 g
Carbohydrates	20.7g
Protein	28.4 g
Cholesterol	49 mg
Sodium	482 mg

Ingredients

1/2 pita bread round
1/4 C. tuna, drained
1/2 dill pickle spear, diced
1 1/2 tsp mayonnaise
1 1/2 tsp olive oil
1/2 tsp garlic powder

1 pinch dried rosemary
1 slice Swiss cheese

Directions

1. Lightly toast the pita bread.
2. Break tuna chunks into small pieces and place into a bowl.
3. Add the pickle, mayonnaise, olive oil, garlic powder and rosemary and mix till well combined.
4. Place Swiss cheese into the pocket of the toasted pita bread, followed by the tuna mixture.
5. In a microwave safe dish, place the pita sandwich and microwave for about 15-20 seconds.

TUNA
Marinara Pasta

🥣 Prep Time: 15 mins

🕐 Total Time: 45 mins

Servings per Recipe: 6	
Calories	544 kcal
Fat	8.2 g
Carbohydrates	85.3g
Protein	33.1 g
Cholesterol	23 mg
Sodium	1001 mg

Ingredients

olive oil
3 cloves garlic, minced
6 large zucchini, cut into 1/2-inch cubes
1 tsp salt
1 tsp dried Italian herb seasoning
1/2 tsp red pepper flakes
1 (28 oz.) jar marinara sauce

1 1/2 C. water
2 (7 oz.) pouches tuna
1 (16 oz.) package elbow macaroni
1 tsp grated Parmesan cheese

Directions

1. In a skillet, heat the olive oil in a skillet on medium heat and sauté the garlic for about 2 minutes.
2. Stir in the zucchini, salt, Italian herbs and red pepper flakes and cook for about 5 minutes.
3. Stir in the marinara sauce and water and bring to a boil.
4. Gently, stir in the tuna and simmer for about 7-10 more minutes.
5. In a large pan of lightly salted boiling water, cook the macaroni for about 7 minutes.
6. Drain well.
7. Add the macaroni into tuna mixture and mix till well combined.
8. Turn off the heat but keep the pan, covered for about 6 minutes and 15 seconds.
9. Serve with a sprinkling of the Parmesan cheese.

Rustic
Tuna Bake

 Prep Time: 30 mins

Total Time: 1 hr 15 mins

Servings per Recipe: 6

Calories	562 kcal
Fat	31.3 g
Carbohydrates	39.9g
Protein	30.8 g
Cholesterol	125 mg
Sodium	793 mg

Ingredients

1/2 C. butter, divided
1 (8 oz.) package uncooked medium egg noodles
1/2 medium onion, finely chopped
1 stalk celery, finely chopped
1 clove garlic, minced
8 oz. button mushrooms, sliced
1/4 C. all-purpose flour
2 C. milk

salt and pepper to taste
2 (6 oz.) cans tuna, drained and flaked
1 C. frozen peas, thawed
3 tbsp bread crumbs
2 tbsp butter, melted
1 C. shredded Cheddar cheese

Directions

1. Set your oven to 375 degrees F before doing anything else and grease a casserole dish with 1 tbsp of the melted butter.
2. In a large pan of lightly salted boiling water, cook the egg noodles for about 8-10 minutes.
3. Drain well.
4. In a skillet, melt 1 tbsp of the butter on medium-low heat and sauté the onion, celery and garlic for about 5 minutes.
5. Increase the heat to medium-high and stir in the mushrooms and stir fry for about 5 minutes.
6. In a medium pan, melt 4 tbsp of the butter and add the flour, beating continuously till smooth.
7. Slowly, add the milk, beating continuously and cook for about 5 minutes.
8. Stir in the tuna, peas, mushroom mixture, salt, pepper and cooked noodles.
9. Transfer the tuna mixture into the prepared casserole dish.

10. In a bowl, mix together the remaining 2 tbsp of the melted butter and bread crumbs.
11. Spread the breadcrumbs mixture over the casserole and sprinkle with the cheese evenly.
12. Cook in the oven for about 25 minutes.

Seattle Inspired
Tuna

Prep Time: 15 mins
Total Time: 35 mins

Servings per Recipe: 6
Calories	230 kcal
Fat	7.6 g
Carbohydrates	21.1g
Protein	18.6 g
Cholesterol	48 mg
Sodium	434 mg

Ingredients

2 (6 oz.) cans tuna, drained and flaked
1 egg, beaten
3/4 C. dry bread crumbs
3 green onions, minced
1 clove garlic, peeled and minced
1 tbsp soy sauce
1 tbsp teriyaki sauce
1 tbsp ketchup

1 tsp sesame oil
1 tsp black pepper
1/2 C. cornmeal
2 tbsp vegetable oil

Directions

1. In a large bowl, add the tuna, egg, bread crumbs, green onions, garlic, soy sauce, teriyaki sauce, ketchup, sesame oil and pepper and mix till well combined.
2. Make about 6 (1-inch thick) patties from the mixture and sprinkle the each with the cornmeal from both sides.
3. In a medium skillet, heat the oil on medium heat and cook the patties for about 5 minutes per side.

TUNA
and Capers

Prep Time: 15 mins
Total Time: 40 mins

Servings per Recipe: 6
Calories   400 kcal
Fat   6.3 g
Carbohydrates   59.6g
Protein   26.6 g
Cholesterol   106 mg
Sodium   181 mg

Ingredients

1 tbsp olive oil
1 onion, chopped
2 cloves crushed garlic
1 tbsp capers
1 (14.5 oz.) can crushed tomatoes
1 tbsp lemon juice
1 tbsp chopped fresh parsley

1/4 tsp red pepper flakes
2 (6 oz.) cans tuna, drained
1 (16 oz.) package dry pasta

Directions

1. In a large sauté pan, heat oil on low heat and sauté the onion and garlic till tender.
2. Stir in the capers, tomatoes, lemon juice, parsley and red pepper flake and simmer gently for about 3 minutes.
3. Fold in the tuna and cook till heated completely.
4. Meanwhile in large pan of the boiling water, prepare the pasta till tender.
5. Drain well.
6. Add the pasta into tuna mixture and stir to combine before serving.

Smoky
Tuna Patties

 Prep Time: 5 mins

Total Time: 25 mins

Servings per Recipe: 2

Calories	395 kcal
Fat	18.7 g
Carbohydrates	27.9g
Protein	28.3 g
Cholesterol	118 mg
Sodium	373 mg

Ingredients

1 (6 oz.) can light tuna in water, drained
1 egg
2/3 C. quick-cooking oats
3 tbsp barbeque sauce
3 tbsp chopped green onion
1/2 tsp hot pepper sauce

1/2 tsp dried savory
1 pinch salt
2 tbsp vegetable oil

Directions

1. In a medium bowl, add the tuna, egg and oats and mix till well combined.
2. Stir in the barbecue sauce, green onion, hot pepper sauce, savory and salt.
3. In a large skillet, heat the oil on medium heat.
4. With a tablespoon, place the tuna mixture into the pan and flatten slightly.
5. Cook for about 3 minutes per side.

NOVEMBER'S
Tuna

🥣 Prep Time: 10 mins
🕐 Total Time: 10 mins

Servings per Recipe: 4
Calories	164 kcal
Fat	6.2 g
Carbohydrates	4.9 g
Protein	21.5 g
Cholesterol	28 mg
Sodium	178 mg

Ingredients

2 (6 oz.) cans solid white tuna packed in water, drained
2 tbsp mayonnaise
1/3 tsp dried dill weed

3 tbsp dried cranberries
salt

Directions

1. In a bowl, add the tuna and with a fork, mash it.
2. Add the mayonnaise and stir to coat evenly.
3. Stir in the dill and cranberries and salt.
4. Serve over the crackers or the bread of your choice.

15 Min
Tuna Lunch

🥣 Prep Time: 5 mins

🕐 Total Time: 15 mins

Servings per Recipe: 4

Calories	235 kcal
Fat	18.3 g
Carbohydrates	5.2g
Protein	13 g
Cholesterol	53 mg
Sodium	93 mg

Ingredients

2 tbsp butter
1 clove garlic, minced
1/3 C. chopped onion
1/3 C. chopped green bell pepper

1 (6 oz.) can tuna, drained and flaked
1 C. sour cream
1 tsp curry powder

Directions

1. In a large pan, melt the butter on medium-low heat and cook the garlic, onions and green pepper till soft, stirring occasionally.
2. Stir in the tuna, sour cream, curry powder, salt and pepper and cook till warmed.
3. Serve immediately.

15 MINUTE
Tuna Dinner

Prep Time: 10 mins
Total Time: 15 mins

Servings per Recipe: 4
Calories	270 kcal
Fat	12 g
Carbohydrates	10.4g
Protein	28.7 g
Cholesterol	51 mg
Sodium	406 mg

Ingredients

1 lb. sashimi grade yellowfin tuna
kosher salt to taste
fresh ground black pepper to taste
1/2 C. Italian seasoned bread crumbs

3 tbsp olive oil

Directions

1. With a sharp knife, cut the tuna into 4 large pieces and season with the salt and pepper.
2. Coat the tuna pieces with bread crumbs from all sides lightly.
3. In a large heavy skillet, heat the olive oil on high heat and sear the tuna for about 1 minute per side.
4. Remove from the pan and cut each piece into 1/4-inch thick slices.
5. Serve with your favorite condiments.

Light Tuna
Biscuits

 Prep Time: 15 mins

Total Time: 30 mins

Servings per Recipe: 8
Calories	448 kcal
Fat	19.3 g
Carbohydrates	49.5g
Protein	18.9 g
Cholesterol	17 mg
Sodium	1188 mg

Ingredients

2 (6 oz.) cans chunk light tuna, drained and flaked
1 tbsp finely chopped onion (optional)
1 tbsp finely chopped celery (optional)
2 tbsp shredded Cheddar cheese

1 tsp dried dill weed
2 tbsp mayonnaise
2 (8 count) cans refrigerated biscuit dough

Directions

1. Set your oven to 350 degrees F before doing anything else.
2. In a bowl, add the tuna, onion, celery, shredded Cheddar cheese, dill and mayonnaise and gently stir to combine.
3. Flatten the biscuit dough into about 1/4-inch thickness.
4. Arrange the 8 flattened biscuits onto an ungreased baking sheet.
5. Place about 3 tbsp of the tuna mixture over each biscuit and top each with another flattened biscuit.
6. Pinch the edges to secure the filling.
7. Cook in the oven for about 15 minutes.

TUESDAY'S
Mustard Tuna

Prep Time: 10 mins

Total Time: 20 mins

Servings per Recipe: 4
Calories	500 kcal
Fat	18.3 g
Carbohydrates	55.4g
Protein	28 g
Cholesterol	58 mg
Sodium	1638 mg

Ingredients

8 oz. uncooked elbow macaroni
2 dill pickles, chopped
6 oz. Colby-Jack cheese, cubed
1 (6 oz.) can albacore tuna in water, drained and
flaked

1/2 C. light mayonnaise
1/2 tsp prepared yellow mustard
1 tsp dill pickle juice

Directions

1. In a large pan of lightly salted boiling water, cook the macaroni for about 7 minutes.
2. Rinse under cold running water and drain well.
3. With the paper towels, pat lightly.
4. In a large bowl, add the macaroni, pickles, cheese, tuna, mayonnaise, and mustard, a splash of pickle juice, salt and pepper.
5. Refrigerate, covered for at least 30 minutes before serving.

Crescent Roll
Tuna Bake

🥄 Prep Time: 10 mins
🕐 Total Time: 35 mins

Servings per Recipe: 8	
Calories	278 kcal
Fat	14.5 g
Carbohydrates	19.3g
Protein	16.8 g
Cholesterol	29 mg
Sodium	578 mg

Ingredients

2 tbsp butter
1 small onion, diced
2 (6 oz.) cans tuna, drained
1 (10 oz.) package frozen mixed vegetables
1 (10.75 oz.) can condensed cream of mushroom soup

1/2 C. shredded Cheddar cheese
1 (8 oz.) package refrigerated crescent rolls

Directions

1. Set your oven to 350 degrees F before doing anything else.
2. In a pan, melt the butter on medium heat and sauté the onions till soft and translucent.
3. Stir in the tuna and frozen vegetables and cook, stirring occasionally for about 5-10 minutes.
4. Stir in the cream of mushroom soup.
5. Transfer the mixture into a 9-inch pie dish and sprinkle with the shredded cheese.
6. Unroll and separate the crescent rolls.
7. Arrange each crescent roll over the tuna mixture with the point facing inward, overlapping slightly.
8. Cook in the oven for about 11-13 minutes.
9. Remove from the oven and keep aside for about 5-10 minutes before cutting and serving.

Made in United States
North Haven, CT
23 November 2021

11423036R00035